Contents

KT-163-652

Some words are printed in bold, **like this.** You can find out what they mean in the glossary. You can also look in the box at the bottom of the page where the word first appears.

ACTION!

Stunt doubles are an essential part of some of the most exciting scenes in films.

What do stunt doubles do?

Stunt doubles are daredevil performers who earn money by executing dangerous tasks in films. They perform stunts that actors cannot do, or are averse to doing, themselves. When audiences watch a film, they are not always watching famous actors. This is because stunt doubles are actually performing the dangerous leaps, jumps, and crashes in films.

Stunt fact!

In *Harry Potter and the Chamber of Secrets* (2002), actor Daniel Radcliffe, who plays Harry Potter, actually hangs from a car 9 metres (30 feet) in the air. Radcliffe did not use a stunt double for that scene because he said it sounded like fun and he wanted to try it!

essential   very important and necessary

ATOMIC

BLE

RSON

Raintree

www.raintreepublishers.co.uk
Visit our website to find out more information about **Raintree** books.

To order:

☎ Phone 44 (0) 1865 888112
🗎 Send a fax to 44 (0) 1865 314091
💻 Visit the Raintree bookshop at **www.raintreepublishers.co.uk** to browse
our catalogue and order online.

First published in Great Britain by
Raintree, Halley Court, Jordan Hill,
Oxford OX2 8EJ, part of Harcourt
Education. Raintree is a registered
trademark of Harcourt Education Ltd.

© Harcourt Education Ltd 2007
First published in paperback in 2007.
The moral right of the proprietor has been asserted.

Editorial: Louise Galpine, Rosie Gordon,
Dave Harris, and Stig Vatland
Design: Victoria Bevan and Bigtop
Picture Research: Mica Brancic and Elaine Willis
Production: Camilla Crask
Originated by Chroma Graphics Pte. Ltd
Printed and bound in China by WKT

10 digit ISBN 1 406 20357 2 (hardback)
13 digit ISBN 978 1 4062 0357 8
11 10 09 08 07
10 9 8 7 6 5 4 3 2 1

10 digit ISBN 1 406 20378 5 (paperback)
13 digit ISBN 978 1 4062 0378 3
12 11 10 09 08
10 9 8 7 6 5 4 3 2 1

**British Library Cataloguing in
Publication Data**
Anderson, Jameson
Stunt double. – (Atomic)
791.4'3'028
A full catalogue record for this book is available
from the British Library.

Acknowledgements

The publishers would like to thank the following
for permission to reproduce photographs: Corbis,
p. **9** (Bettmann); Courtesy of The Rocketman aka Ky
Michaelson, pp. **16 (top** and **bottom**); Rex Features,
6 main (Simon Roberts); Ronald Grant Archive, pp. **5**,
20; The Kobal Collection, pp. **6 inset** (Bob Marshak/New
Line/Roger Birnbaum), **19** (Canal/Portobello Pictures),
24 (Jay Maidment/EON/MGM), **13** (Jay Maidment/
MGM/Maverick), **23** (Jay Maidment/Original Films), **27
inset** (Phil Bray/Universal), **11** (United Artists), **28 top**,
28 bottom (Wing Nut Films/Universal); Warner Bros
courtesy The Kobal Collection, p. **27 main**; Scott A Leva,
Precision Stunts, pp. **15 (top** and **bottom**).
Cover: Getty (Photographer's Choice/Chad Ehlers).

The publishers would like to thank Diana Bentley,
Nancy Harris, and Dee Reid for their assistance in the
preparation of this book.

Every effort has been made to contact copyright holders
of any material reproduced in this book. Any omissions
will be rectified in subsequent printings if notice is given
to the publishers.

Disclaimer

Do not try to copy any of the stunts in this book. They are dangerous and should only be done by professional stunt doubles.

Stunt doubles provide a lot of the exciting action in popular films.

Arnold Schwarzenegger's stunt double needs to be nearly the same height and weight as the actor.

Jackie Chan has appeared in more than 65 films.

Hollywood

LOOK-ALIKES

Stunt doubles in films attempt to resemble the actors they portray.

Fooling the audience

Film **directors** hire make-up artists and costume designers to transform stunt people to look like famous actors. When a stunt double closely resembles an actor, the film audience never detects the difference.

The real thing

However, some actors, such as Daniel Radcliffe, sometimes perform their own stunts. Others, such as actor, **martial artist**, and stuntman Jackie Chan, almost always do their own stunts. One of his most famous stunts was when he hung by an umbrella from the door handle of a bus in *Police Story* (1985).

director	someone who is in charge of making sure a film goes as planned
martial artist	person who is an expert at fighting techniques from East Asia, such as karate
portray	look and act like

FAKE FIGHTS

Fight scenes are a major part of a stunt double's job.

Are all fights fake?

Today's film fight scenes do not include any actual punches. Punches and kicks might **graze** the actor, but they do not actually injure anyone.

In old **Westerns**, many fight scenes were real. This is because **directors** in the past believed that real scenes looked better and more realistic. Often stunt doubles were injured in fights, getting black eyes or even losing teeth.

Stunt fact!

Throughout his career, Chuck Robertson worked as **legendary** actor John Wayne's stunt double. In the Western *Hondo* (1953), when an army trooper character shoots at a Native American character, Robertson is playing both roles!

graze	barely make contact
legendary	very well-known
Western	type of film set in the western United States that often features cowboys

Rory Calhoun throws a real punch at Dean Jagger in the Western *Red Sundown* (1956).

FAKE BLOOD

Fake blood helps to make a fake punch look real. When stunt doubles are "hit", they bite down on small capsules filled with fake blood. As the blood flows out of their mouth, the audience believes they have really been hit.

Gunshot!

Stunt doubles also use fake blood to **simulate** being shot. They secure small wires under their clothes. On one side of the wire is a capsule filled with fake blood, and on the other side is a **detonator**. The detonators are used to send electricity to the capsules. This makes the capsules explode causing the fake blood to flow, which makes the gunshot look genuine.

Stunt fact!

Jackie Chan lost real blood when his tooth was accidentally kicked out in *Snake in the Eagle's Shadow* (1978).

Fake blood is mostly corn syrup and food colouring.

capsule	shell that contains a fluid or medicine inside
detonator	tool that makes something explode
simulate	act like you are doing something

BANG!

Some of the most spectacular film scenes are those involving explosions. Stunt doubles make these scenes look authentic by flying through the air.

How stunt doubles fly

Stunt doubles usually use an **air ram** in explosion scenes. An air ram is a small platform that uses air pressure to rapidly throw someone into the air. When there is an explosion in a film, air rams propel the stunt doubles high into the air.

Stunt fact!

The most expensive explosion scene in a film occurred in 2001's *Pearl Harbor*. The bombing of warships cost £2.9 million. During the scene, six ships were destroyed. The scene took one month to set up and was filmed by twelve camera crews.

air ram   stunt tool that uses air pressure to throw someone up in the air

Air rams throw actors or stunt doubles away from the explosion.

POW!

When a person is shot, the force of the bullet drives them backwards. When a fast-moving bullet hits a person in a film, the audience expects the actor to also be forced backwards.

How to fake being shot

An **air ratchet** is used to pull stunt actors backwards so that their movements look real. They wear special **harnesses** under their clothing, and the harnesses are connected to an air ratchet. The air ratchet pulls the stunt double away from the action so it appears as if he really has been shot.

air ratchet	stunt tool that uses air to pull stunt doubles backwards
harness	piece of equipment that fits around a person's body and holds the person in place

Achieving the perfect air ratchet stunt takes training and practice.

Bruce Brown, who organized stunts for the *Lord of the Rings* films, used an air ratchet like this to make it look like a character could leap 12 metres (40 feet) in the air.

Dar Robinson fell
at a speed of up to
9.8 metres (32 feet)
per second.

Over the Edge

Mountain-climbing gear helps keep stunt doubles safe. When they plummet or are pushed from a structure, stunt doubles are sometimes connected to ropes and cables. This equipment prevents them from hitting the ground.

Climbers and fallers

Ropes and cables might not be necessary in some circumstances. This is because stunt doubles can also make use of air mats, nets, or trampolines to cushion their fall.

Stunt fact!

In the 1984 film *Highpoint*, stuntman Dar Robinson leapt from a height of about 335 metres (1,100 feet). Jumping from the CN Tower in Toronto, Canada, Robinson was attached to the tower by a small cable and landed safely on a parachute stretched on the ground. He was paid £80,000 for the stunt.

PLAYING WITH FIRE

Fire cannot be controlled the way other stunts can. Stunt **coordinators** can tell exactly where people will land when they jump from a window, but they cannot determine exactly how a fire will burn.

How do stunt doubles stay safe?

To protect themselves from fire, stunt doubles wear fireproof suits and cover themselves in fire-protective gels. Fire burns on the gel, but does not harm the skin of the stunt double.

Stunt fact!

In 2004, stuntman Ted A. Batchelor burned his whole body for 2 minutes, 38 seconds. He used a special gel on his clothes that prevented his skin from being burned. Only experienced stunt people should attempt a stunt like this.

coordinator   person who plans something ahead of time

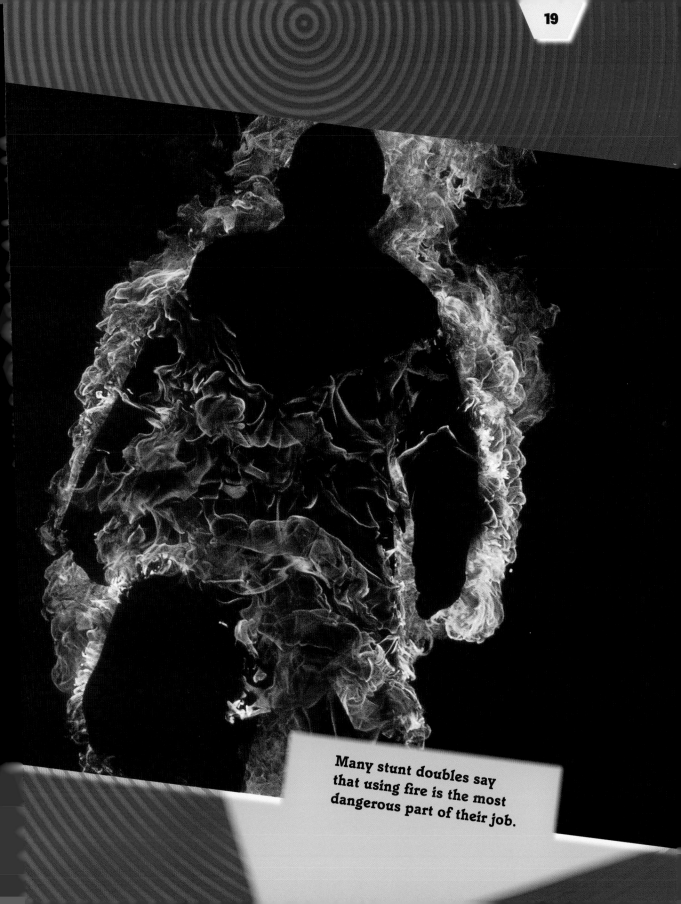

Many stunt doubles say
that using fire is the most
dangerous part of their job.

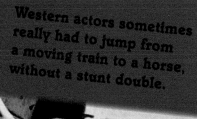

Western actors sometimes really had to jump from a moving train to a horse, without a stunt double.

stagecoach — vehicle used in the 1800s that had a closed cabin on wheels that was pulled by horses. It was used by travellers and mail carriers.

transfer — move from one place to another

All Aboard!

During **transfer** stunts, stunt doubles move from one object to another, usually while both objects are in motion. Transfer stunts are some of the most frequent stunts in films.

Dangerous leaps

Since the earliest films, stunt doubles have worked on aeroplanes. Stunt doubles who perform transfer stunts on aeroplanes are also called wing walkers. Ormer Locklear earned the nickname "King of the Wing Walkers" in 1920. He later gained fame as one of the film industry's finest stunt pilots.

Transfer stunts were also popular in old **Westerns**, when cowboys jumped from their horse to a moving **stagecoach** or train.

Stunt fact!

Western actor Jack Williams had a horse called Coco that could lie down and play dead as if it had been shot.

TRANSFER STUNTS

Today's actors are more likely to take part in **transfer** stunts with cars. They sometimes have to leap from one moving car to another.

How to do a transfer stunt

The drivers play a vital role in transfer stunts. Both vehicles must be moving at the same speed and must be driven smoothly. This makes transfer from one vehicle to another much more straightforward. Only trained stunt people should ever attempt this type of stunt!

Stunt fact!

The film *Cliffhanger* (1993), starring Sylvester Stallone, included some of the most expensive stunts ever. In one scene, stuntman Simon Crane leapt from one jet to another 4,572 metres (15,000 feet) in the air. Due to the cost of using the jets, the stunt cost £533,000 to film.

This transfer stunt is from *The Fast and the Furious* (2001).

In this car chase scene from *Die Another Day* (2002), James Bond drives an Aston Martin V12 that in the film can become invisible.

CAR CHASES

In addition to driving fast, stunt doubles also have to make their cars jump, roll over, and crash.

Stunt cars

What film audiences may not realize is that the cars used in these scenes are special stunt-driving cars. In many stunt cars, the interior of the car has been modified to be more like a race car. Often a driver is strapped in with a full **harness**, which protects him during a roll-over scene. Stunt drivers also wear helmets when they drive.

Stunt fact!

The longest car jump in a film is from *Smokey and the Bandit II*. In this 1980 film, a car travelling at 128 kilometres (80 miles) per hour jumped 49.6 metres (163 feet).

CRASH AND ESCAPE

Stunt drivers sometimes have to **simulate** escaping from cars that have crashed or been driven off bridges into water.

Escaping with their lives

All vehicles that are sent under water contain aquatic breathing devices. These air tanks enable a stunt double to breathe while under water. The vehicles also have an escape **hatch** for the stunt double to escape through.

Stunt fact!

During the filming of the TV programme *The Dukes of Hazzard*, 309 Dodge Chargers were used and crashed. Only about 20 of the stunt cars exist today; they are very valuable.

hatch   small door

For underwater car stunts, boats are anchored just outside of the camera's view to help if the stunt person has any trouble.

A scene is often filmed with only an actor.
A computer-generated background and
special effects are then added later.

INTO THE FUTURE

The future of stunt work in films will probably involve computers in addition to actors. New technology allows computer programmers and graphic artists to create scenes that look real, without putting stunt doubles in peril.

New stunts

In early films stunt doubles were often in more danger than those working today. As films have changed, so has the nature of the profession. Today's stunt doubles are skilled people who train and prepare for their stunts, and are therefore able to carry them out safely.

Even though computers are becoming increasingly useful for creating stunt scenes, stunt doubles and stunt **coordinators** will always work in films. They will always be needed to make sure that each new action film has stunts more daring and exciting than the last.

Glossary

air ram stunt tool that uses air pressure to throw someone up in the air

air ratchet stunt tool that uses air to pull stunt doubles backwards

capsule shell that contains a fluid or medicine inside

coordinator person who plans something ahead of time

detonator tool that makes something explode

director someone who is in charge of making sure a film goes as planned. The director also guides the creative elements of a film.

essential very important and necessary

graze barely make contact

harness piece of equipment that fits around a person's body and holds the person in place

hatch small door

legendary very well-known

martial artist person who is an expert at fighting techniques from East Asia, such as karate

portray look and act like

simulate act like you are doing something

stagecoach vehicle used in the 1800s that had a closed cabin on wheels that was pulled by horses. It was used by travellers and mail carriers.

transfer move from one place to another

Western type of film set in the western United States that often features cowboys

Want to know more?

Books

✳ *Star Files: Jackie Chan*, Dan Fox (Raintree, 2005)

✳ *Stunt Double*, Aileen Weintraub (Children's Press, 2003)

✳ *Stunt Performers*, Tony Hyland (Smart Apple, 2006)

Websites

✳ www.guinnessworldrecords. com/content_pages/record. asp?recordid=50603
This website tells you about some of the record-breaking stunts carried out in films.

If you liked this Atomic book, why don't you try these...?

Index

Notes for adults
Use the following questions to guide children towards identifying features of explanation text:

Can you find an example of a main heading and side heading on page 4?
Can you give examples of two connectives from page 8?
Can you find two examples of the present tense on page 10?
Can you find the different steps taken to fake being shot on page 14?
Can you give examples of side headings starting with 'how' and 'what'?